life is
everything

life is everything

everything

the thoughtful collection I

jolene parke

ISBN: 9798478152000

i dedicate this book
to the thoughtful
who are raw with
their words
the ones whose truth
speaks revival
into existence

healing can be from stepping
out & into the wilderness...

the aperture in the
thin paper walls
the streets brim with
rambling boomboxes
in a dingbat city
studio apartment
attending frequent parties
while home alone abstinent
without an rsvp or invitation
blocks of musical sirens
patrol making me feel safe
with their holsters strapped
mixing sounds & cocktails

now i am comforted
soft feet damp in moss
grounding amid croon cricket
lullabies in the storybook forest
conflicting sounds from memory
terrarium home, my rock

-trying to break the trauma bond

don't be fearful
for you are stardust
the stars prevail
through holes
they are glimpses
of our home
where we came from
twinkling keepsakes
don't be fearful
the sun is here with you
you are the warmth
you are the light
you are stardust

life is short
live today as so
but my life is long
it's a bending road
365 days of waking
with years to come
at stints a straight road
in which the good days
make up for the bad
& tomorrow i am needed
as long as i am here
there is meaning
in an intentionally long life
with the promise
to a generous impact
forthcoming offerings
imminent beginnings
as long as i am present
today is everything

-life is everything

take the time
to love yourself
silence out others
who have hurt you
during this period
i have learned
that you can heal

i write so that you fall in love
you read to fall in love
that's what poetry is
a love story

if i look hindmost
back to the me
that was silly
at the uneven age of
thirteen
an oddly butterfly
stage of growth
i will find my life transform
for the first time
as per first flutter
surrounded by the enchantment
of lisa frank
i will ask for its fairylike essence
to stay with me
through & through this life

this new year i want to be seen
i want to be understood
i want my circumstances to be valid
as reasons as to why i am
& where i am today
i want this new year to be
the beginning of trust
in love
in who & where i can go
with endless possibilities
hard work & passion
i want to be given the chance
to live my dreams
& not let fate slip out of my fingers
due to things that are out of my
control
i want you to see me
& my unforgettable love for you
through it all
this year i want all the possibilities

be inspired by
creation
& always live
within
your purpose

bless the wind
that helps *me feel*

befriend your
spirit
in a realm
of lost souls

the indigo ocean
gets murkier
the deeper you explore
so i stay afloat the turquoise

the passion to grow
is the seeker
in the opportunist
the will to become
is the chancer
believing that
we are all thinking
the same familiarities
as fragile beings
meant to live curiously

resilient beings are familiar
with pain
it's what makes them sensitive
they had to be sympathetic
to themselves
comfort their aching
living amongst the beauty
in a setting
as they require the comfort
never seeking drama
still finding themselves there
as an outcome of kindness
one who doesn't try to mend
befalls prey to the oppressor
questioning your oneself
as your energy is taken from you
to be inherently strong
is to not impersonate nor
hold close to your heart the antagonism

-hurt can only live if you give it oxygen

sometimes your life
does not feel
like your own
because
you lose yourself
in everyone

silence your devil
flutter your wings

emotions are revealed in all babies
crying unrestricted at birth
but in the rooted adult self
a display of weeping willow tears
are taught to be concealed
strength is shown in the constriction
of sentiments spilling out so easily
but we still need to have a release
so that we can emotionally regulate
for when we do not feel
we allow this new body to harden

-why do we punish the inner child

maroon & emerald
marzipan swirled plants
a stationary reflection
of nature in its golden state
a sunbathing gilded lake
painted greeneries
spread out unevenly
sprouted babies
from the stem branches
with dark blond shrubberies
the skin of a ripened pear
fluorescent leaves budding
round plump crowns
sweet bouquets of
sour green apple balm
if you are patient
you can taste the seasons
changing their colors

-the beginning of spring

it's ok that you didn't
follow your dreams

-not all dreams were meant to be lived

rise with the sun
it is *awakening*
the world

what is life but a passing day
one that you live to reminisce in
trying to distinguish
to make sense of it
solving the unknown by reiterating
the journeys that you once lived
as the memories jolt through your mind
you start to see the sensations
feel the reactions over
they help you determine
how you will resume
you are knowingly forming
future glimpses into the unknown
with every recollected self-reflection
i like to think that i can
bring into existence through echoing

i am inspired
by the bottomless blue ocean
why it is the color sapphire
a navy diamond in the rough
how the stars
'oomph'
in a silken lustrous glossed sky
the way the wind chooses to storm
in whichever direction it feels
& what sentiment the force composes
as it plays with my hair
the ordinary that we do not question
the why
to what we gather every day
what the clouds seem to be hiding
a beautiful veil
from beyond this sphere
the shapeshifting recurrences
they recreate for us
& how it all somehow
becomes the effects of fluoride on us

-a wonderful world that we know nothing about

it's not that this person wants to
see you at your worst
mirroring how unloved they feel
bestowed onto you as hurt & pain

it is the way that they see themselves
for when you are happy without them
they want you to be unhappy as well

not because they do not love you
but because *they think that they do*

-broken hearts become heartbreakers

kaleidoscopic cluster crystals
hanging in sunlit rooms
disco ball mornings with you
twinkling warm vanilla bulbs
baking our home sweeter
aurora borealis in the north
coconut ginger toothpaste
naturally bleached teeth
simplicity puts me at ease
something about our vows
forever wanting you
kindergarten kind-hearted
towels with engraved initials
linen layers perfectly crumpled
changing positions with you
the same way you make me feel
a virgin in wedding dress lingerie
every evening since i said

- "i do" my love

if fear is the devil
then faith is in
falling

the biggest regret
is taking for granted
the gift of wellness
only when you are sick
do you pray to feel better

-holistic is a form of self-care

it is not
who you are
it is
a choice

-choices define you

she was perfect
but to only the eye of the beholder
& that was her problem

-she never believed she was worthy

pursue your rare self
the part that makes you
irreplicable
share what inspires
& benefits you to others

-you were you before you were born

only in the end
when the credits roll
will you understand

watching our movie on repeat
trying to rewind your mistakes

-how i wish we were still filming

ripping the bandage
is scary
because it exposes you
but it also
takes you out of the dark

if they want help
provide for them
if they cannot
help themselves
then guide them

we are brought into the world
with the learned ideology
that we will become
something
even though we cannot
grasp who we are
we become our storyline
we lose ourselves
in our predicaments
through traumatic experiences
that become understandings
i have found that our talent
has always resided inside of us

-be your guardian & you will bloom

i am kept awake
by the pull of the moon
amongst the abstruse clouds
filled mysteriously
with unpredictable lightning bolts
the swing seat that hangs
off the tipping golden hue
of half the moon
with my feet dangling irresponsibly
gripping the sides
of the heavenly
radiant linear strings
i am consumed with the burden
of the world beneath me
so much that i can neither
sleep nor dream

when you try to please your
youthful innermost self
you will see yourself
in a tantrum
but if you can let go
of the adolescent figure
that you lived
become the adult
who carries the weight
then you can allow yourself
to be a child at heart again
where the wholesome originated

-adulthood is something we have to mentally grow into

she held her own future
calling on the pull
of the opaque black waves
wishing wholly on every star
she made her dreams a reality
with moonbeams

be thankful for what
you cannot see
the universe
is your friend
with eyes wide open

keep your heart light
& when the world
leaves you empty
fill your heart
with love for yourself

getting older
is feeling trapped
in your body
in your own skin
but toughened

trust *no one*
who trusts
no one

look upon troubles as
distractions to your mind
try to focus on
what you can control
guard your soul barrier
preserve your heart

-try to do this by not wandering endlessly

the heart can be a muse
for your dreams
glittery meditative notions
that compliment you
reading fictional literature
can create a yearning vision
fantasies can be a form of coping
the beautiful should ponder harder
maybe settle for a *simpler glimmer*

we fear to change
when in actuality
each circadian routine is different
a new date this calendar year
we are change
it is the structure of our everyday lives
the misconception is that
we have control over our decisions
in a way of living
that we already endure

-trust in the paths that the universe opens up to you

we keep the dominant pain
concealed within our identities
undisclosed cracks
that we think are secure
but that remains vulnerable
we don't realize it is a silhouette
that shadows our shadow
the less you speak about it
the wilder it grows
the smaller you are in essence
let yourself cry a rainstorm
that destroys you
then become friends with the storm
let it heal you as it becomes you
& makes you stronger
arching a beautiful rainbow

-with it comes the release of trauma

now i remember
why i befriended fame
when normal
becomes a lie too

how do we get people
to care
when life feels too short

your bed is devised to
center your thoughts
a safe haven to dream
wide arms aligned
extended effortlessly
fingertips reaching the
ends of the mattress
turning your head sideways
laying parallel to a massage
pulling on heartstrings
arms cuddling in self-love
the sheets concealing you
falling backward in trust
on to the softest era
what we should feel
the comfort we long for

-a place to lay our weary heads

the air smelled of bumblebee
heated pollen blossoms
an orangish crushed sun
clinique happy eau de parfum
millennial pink beach cruisers
shimmering wet bikinis
dripping downwards
onto skinny tires
reflecting pedals
day pastels
periwinkle skies
darker shades at dusk
grass made jewelry
ethereal lit fireflies
frost lipstick
butterfly crop tops
bejeweled denim
clinging to tawny skin
reusable ice cubes
frozen flavored freeze pops
soda-lime glass bottles
between inner thigh gaps
inflatables stagnant in chlorine
neighboring night games
unruly chaperoned house parties
postmidnight kisses in parked cars
prancing sprinklers on every front yard

-summertime's ago

sometimes the fire
in me
is so strong
that it backfires
& burns all
that is around me

-why do i care so much

the soul
it has no face
just the mirror
tells time

the sorrow in a dream
that never dies
when you are still living
without it

gratuity is expected
at an expensive place
but gratitude comes from
an inexpensive place

in a man's world
he rules by patriarchy
women must be grace
females focus on maintaining
their exterior
men living through
their exterior
in a world where she exists
to cater to an ego
that she will never understand

if life was truly
black & white
then why
do we live in color

there is no true entity
as ethereal beauty
when one model
can become another
within symmetry

-we are all becoming the same

the body is a vessel
that allows
the soul to hide

i do not have a choice
existing in an world
mass-produced
with immoral choices
leaving behind
decisions
we only hope can be reversed
i ask you to reconsider
so that all of us can
inhabit where we belong

-dear society

each day is a depiction
of your reality
you are swatching the pigments
every second you are alive
if you look back
you can view the masterpiece
if you look to the future
remember that you started
with a blank canvas
& you can still choose
to paint from scratch

the truth behind a secret
is not a truth
but a falsehood

-a white lie is really black

you are rememberable
inside people's hearts

you know it's
an *addiction*
when you cannot
stop doing
what you know
you need to break
even more
than you did
yesterday

awoken is standing outside
of the body
viewing yourself heartlessly bruised
actually seeing it
from another's perspective

-this is when you start to heal

you keep voiced thoughts
in a seashell locket choker
resembling a little mermaid
who has lost her ability
to speak
steadfast for slender legs
neglecting your intellect
instead of swimming
you acquired to walk
when all you had to do
was sing to your own song

-they say to be careful what you wish for

the sleepless rain of the night
fun in a vibrant afterglow
luminous street decorations
showcasing watercolors
picturesque puddles
mary poppins chalk drawings
hopping into a wonderland
of wavering dim lights
blinking stricken signs
the hush in the dawn
raging music that starts the evening
instruments that serenade the night
we are different beings at nightfall
we are mushroom heads
open to the hallucinations
the nocturnal animals we are
they scatter past
indulging in the camouflaged darkness
the crisp sound of the nature imprint
when all is in a stagnant habitation
of stillness with creation
the clock pulsates on in the after-hours
but we are infinite in the night

secrets stay when we
cannot utter of them
be kind to yourself
by being sincere
words of truth will set you free
take revenge in speaking
of what seems a relic
but even as you rebuild
it was you & you are still
by sharing
you can give a piece away
no one is taking any more
from your heart
the more vulnerable you are
with your autobiography
the more who can relate
further you'll be in healing
until you don't feel the need
to relive it
secrets can cripple your soul
if left as a secret

-the healing journey

never would you have trusted me
if you did not forgive
those who hurt you

without faith in humanity
never would you
have invested in getting to know me

never would you have
loved me harder
without the strength from heartache

never would you
have found love though
without always choosing it

-love can surprise you with more love

it sulks hereafter in a death
within dusty items of stale
never lived in
with price tags hanging
attached still to their belongings
entwined in reminiscences
of nostalgia
we all must not be bound
to living for possessions
that we leave behind *haunted*

a steaming bath in the winter
dulled from the cold air
leaking in from the front porch
wooden wicks
pure beeswax candles
sparkle lit amid gray clouds
standing up bare
bubbles shell your skin
with still water rippling
angelic snowy covers melt you
interwoven chunky knit throws
silk lavender covers at dusk
to slip into an unruffled sleep

- your life is a cup of tea

if you judge too much
your life will be a courtroom

breakaway when you sense
in your gut
that your prayers are *answered*

when you are sure
keep on seeking
for some things never come
as they are
& other times
they never actually come at all

-i was told once to never make an assumption

running in place
an endless scenery
that she fears to inhabit
all her dreams
live behind her eyelids
until she awakens to them

-believe it's already yours

the worst part of living
is in dying
you are forced to dive into it

-you are not swimming anymore

she's an extrovert
but she wants
to be *hidden*

every day i am
less ignorant
then the day before
but if this is not
accurate
i undoubtedly
have regrets
for not questioning
my missteps

mistakes happen
innocent traps
unintentionally
thoughtless choices
become another's fate
i never meant it
yet i am accountable
for the irreparable
chain of circumstances
i have caused a lasting
domino effect

what does it mean
to be happy?
how do i trust happiness
when it is momentary
the philosophy in happily ever after
am i really happy?
happiness is a passing moment
just as desire
a belief can alter
love can falter
it is a promise of a means of living
if you want to be happy
then let it be your perception

maybe where the sun
tints the horizon
a golden halo
is where you peek
from heaven
as a daily reminder
of a better place
while blessing me
every day from a distance

-I feel you beaming down on me

the need for approval
the perfectionist
but what happens when
the person you breathe in
only glorifies your culpabilities
instead of empowering you
for your loveliness
trusting in only your imperfections
relying on this person
for without their analysis
faults will be made
if only met with self-love
without such annotations
there would not be a need
to listen to anyone else

-emotional abuse

she likes when it fades
ombre crimson at eve
an elysian fire sundown
ruby wilting to mulberry
a tinsel sunset disc
touching the view
in her field of vision
she radiates inside
to the blushing sky
holding all her wishes
she smears her course
in mauve pixie dust that
keeps her free from reality

remember to
act quickly
in life
lessons learned
are better *than lost*

life is too short to risk
unless it is out of love
only for love
do we die
within heaven's ways

it is that one thing
that meant nothing
then
means nothing still
yet you think about it
every now & then
you will never understand
why it has stuck with you
for all these years

easing into restlessness
surrendering to the moon
gazing to the bright side
to not feel lonesome
but overwhelmed
by all the others
i have to share you with
no matter how beautifully
you glowed for me

-i could never look at you the same

love is built
it's a sturdy deck
attached & leaning
against the house
a consistent friendship
to stand together with
only then can it
cultivate into a home

when the moon becomes whole
as do the positive thoughts
& dreams you release into the universe

some live for a dream that
they refuse to walk down
a spiral staircase of stardust
obligated to stay high
searching for the castle
holding on to imagination
not allowing the ground
to stimulate their fall
others are down-to-earth
they walk about knowing
that they cannot fall
not looking up to the stars
deeming it acceptable
some can aspire to reality
while others can only wish

there is not enough time
for me to love you
the way i wish i had
through years bewildered
in a city
the family cul-de-sac
cookie cutter suburbs
thousands of lakes
timeless evergreen pine trees
are all calling me back home

-full cycle

when in your safe place
you can be yourself
even when you are
still learning who that is
it may not feel safe
to be vulnerable
but you must try
so that others can love you

the loneliest person
is always looking
for a friend in the mirror

-selfies & self-love

at times all the rivers
can seem like one
walking beside the creek
as a child from losing my way
i remember jumping the waves
while holding my father's hand
amidst the california strand
meeting novel water for the first time
the oceans seem to be the same
we are all connected
to the bodies of water
that individually run through us
every tear that sheds
all seems like one big human despair
but the water also washes us clean
we are sparkling in the rain
i remember the thunderstorm
that flashed white
i closed my eyes as the sky went bright

i want to exist
in where the end of the day
goes down smoothly
drinking a pink moscato sunset
till i am bubbly
princess in a rouge rosarium
showcasing our love
that's where i want to see you again
on a citrine yellow night
staying up late thinking about you
off the path of a deserted road
a full moon illumining the pool
outlining a shiny ring
the beginning of a romance
at a drive-in theater
the crescent moon is crystal clear
amid the fluffed-up clouds
the stars on the screen twinkle
along with the stars overhead

-he said will you run away with me & i wanted to say yes

how could we
come to fathom
that being happy
is a birthright
when destructive
in a bad state of mind
we conceal the freedom
we behold
therefore it seems hard
to believe in ourselves
& *in being happy*

the beach is a place
that will never go outdated
a sunken porthole
to the pearly gates
the alluring ocean takes in
all suppressed feelings
washing thoughts absent
broken down into
polished crystallized
sand particles
shorelines warming your heart
serenity in the coastal sun
solace in sweeping sunsets
let the sea salt restore
yourself to a new moon

if the bad cards
were given to you
as the dealer
to deal out
then your future
was dealt
before the game began
there is nothing
for you to gamble

-that's life

at a diner in a quaint town
that you have to drive through
to get to *getting over you*
playing country blues tracks
the melody is all you can hear
staring at the silverware display
cowboys encircling you
the song balances into the chatter
your thoughts become quieter
closing your eyes
taking in all the melancholy
that you suffered in chorus
together with the musical lyrics

-the therapy session is over

I lived more
than i settled
survived with scars
ascended higher
than imagined
now i can slow down
as i continue to develop
into a better person

-retrospective

the tides awaken the sea
generously letting us swim
amongst its ferocity
when the whitecaps crash hard
they appear to catch the light
an iridescent piercing knife
the marine is reggae
blanketing a seashell haven
jewelry of the briny
inhaling & exhaling
through the gills
the surf equilibrium
a vintage gem comes to life
sun pecked by the intensity
blue hues glistening

fake smiles plastered
permanently on someone
who lacks empathy
real smiles distinctly imprinted
in kindness with age
seen in the presence of love
from smiling for others
that should not be normalized

-rare smiles are real smiles

give someone a chance
an honest rope to catch
a diamond to hold
& they will cultivate a power
in the responsibility
over the chaos of survival
with a little bit of hope
curates a prevailing devotion
to do everything the right way

we are not here to be right
we are here to live
within the fleetingness
neither are we here
to purposely do any wrong
but we need purpose
to prevail over our sins
suffering cannot be taken back
forgiveness only conceals

when warped angels
neglect love
they are frightened of good
attacking their world
making it smaller
be their guardian angel

-watch over them from afar

they will sell to you
convince you that you're
something you are not
to make you purchase
what you did not know
you needed
then you show it off to others
a trend is instigated
as others copy
led by the forefront of fabrications
spun out of control
by the populace
radically unaware of their choices
you might think you are
cherry-picking
but you are only accepting
from the options given to you
the world spins
we intuitively adopt

when your world
becomes still
you can meet yourself
for you are obligatory
to be stationary
remaining doors are closed
they keep you innocent
at peace with your
misbehaved scars
deprived of what
doesn't have substance
anymore
what you exist on now
are balanced thoughts
a silver lining
higher frequency
practicing inwards
before outwardly
their is a kindness there
that has yet to be felt

-a genuine love for yourself

always hold on to
your light
as you have sweet dreams
even though it's dark
all around you

twisted tales
our
love stories

the foundation
of first love
is cultured by family

she was in love with
her mistakes
so she kept making them

power is useless
when revenge
is served
in response to
evil tendencies
& the misuse defines
who you have become

i cannot be honey
if i am
swarmed by bees

-but i can kill with kindness

when you do not
know
let your heart decide
it is your gut
it is your divinity

do not rely on chance
but have faith in the willing

-show me that you love me

isn't the steady line
reassuring now
after the peak
peaceful is
the heavy realization
that all will simply
just be ok

-grateful

scrutinizing a photo
that i took of myself
viewing it as unattractive
i sought justness in the
amount of attempts
i could succeed at it
the failure to accept
the beauty that is there
unlike the ugliness of
someone conceited
for to be vain you must
think highly of yourself
so if i am not arrogant
then what idiocy is left?

-there must be beauty in our insecurities

the black isolated sky
looks down
the exposed window
it halts the brilliance
with dimness
turning off the light
letting the darkness in
i have become one
with the nightfall

-i will not be scared

when you deserve better
you cannot be a victim
to the wrongdoing
not become skeptical
of all that brings you sorrow
for in your dismay
it is easy to sit quietly
but you will still be a target
for hate in silence
you warrant what you allow
to convey in your head
speak only highly of yourself
do not allow others' words
to taint your opinion of yourself

please do not
block out the bad
by closing inwards

- keep on going with me

depression is the trees
deprived of squall
lined up aside power lines
the grumbling sounds
of an empty stomach
stuffed gluttony
the darkness becomes relief
as insomnia trickles in
letting the next day go by unlived
invisible barriers that isolate you
walls that move inwards
boxing you in with the taste
of reckless decisions
fascinating your psyche
easily bothered by sounds
yet you cannot endure
the silence alone
nor quietly with another
they say depression kills
but it destroys from within
& *the inside cannot be seen*

when life does not
make sense
savor the moments
in which it did
embrace your history
as you choose
your battles wisely

rumor has it that
if what was said
is your truth
then you have failed
to do your due diligence
what a tribulation it is
to fill in the blanks with gossip

-don't let me be misunderstood

how do i know that you'll be ok?
because you did today before
& *today is just another yesterday*

you continue to play
with your marbles
but
you are losing them

ignorance
is bliss
but it has its
timestamp

if the earth is our mother
do we not respect our elders?
we must take care
of what once took care of us

apprehension reasoning
stops us from living
but there is a purpose
when it protects
by listening to
the inner voice of our
covert subconscious
keeping us safe

-carefully guiding us to fate

the curl of my hand seduces
as my waist curves
into my hips
my drawn-out-body arches
to the symphony of atoms
orbiting midair
that pulls my body weightless
a lighthearted gravitational balance
the figure is a frame
that connects to our sensuality
with it a release of mutual desire

-dancing with you

when you have nothing
everything
will always be enough

one day mama i won't look like this
i'll look a little more like you
with the strength you fought for
the scars you can't tell me about
with the beauty you forgot is still in you
i look to the mirror to find you daily
i think i have something to look forward to
with every step you taught me
how to be like you
just like you taught yourself
i never walked alone through life
but neither did you mama
i was always a shadow behind taking notes
writing them into time
i hope to follow every one of your steps
even the ones you're not proud of
for your mistakes made me stronger
& you always said regrets are the worst
you don't have to hold onto any pain
you let it go when you birthed me
i will forever be your bundle of joy
you'll always be a mother & a daughter
& i'll always be your daughter
walking just one step behind you

all poetry the same
is written & read
by a dreamer

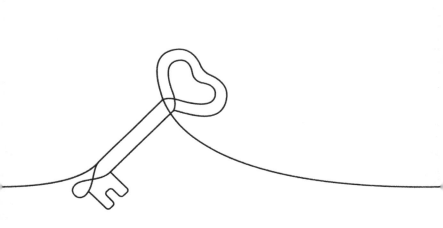

acknowledgments

i am grateful for the evolution that this book has given me.
hoping it simultaneously grows new branches once read.
the same as therapy, these are words to get you through life.

thank you for letting my words become consumed.

with deep intentions on the go
while living in los angeles
came penned poetry, sitting with me.
i found all had a common thread in life.

the thoughtful collection is a thoughtful friend.

life is everything
being the first of three books in
the thoughtful collection.

social media: @writtenbyjolene | linktree

Made in the USA
Monee, IL
05 November 2024

68617591R00077